Merry Christmas Fred

This is a possible
treasure - Hope that
doesn't diminish the
pleasure -
Love, Renate

STOCKHOLM

ISBN 91-85500-12-7

ISBN 91-85500-11-9 (Swedish edition)
ISBN 91-85500-13-5 (German edition)
© Text: Per Anders Fogelström
   Photo: Åke Mokvist
Translated by Paul Britten Austin
Produced by Åke Mokvist for Svenska Bokhandlarföreningen.
Stockholm 1979

This book is printed in offset by Ljunglöfs Offset AB, Stockholm,
on Scheufelen Phönix Imperial 150 g, and Mo-Do Offblade 150 g.
Colour separations by laser scanner, by Kå-Pe Grafiska, Stockholm.
Typesetting on an IBM 82 Composer using 11/13 p Press Roman Medium.
Binding: Bonniers Grafiska Industrier AB, Stockholm.
All photos were taken with a Nikon camera.
Colour film: Kodachrome and Ektachrome.

STOCKHOLM

Text: Per Anders Fogelström
Photo: Åke Mokvist

Svenska Bokhandlareföreningen

Stockholm

Stockholm is a city sprung from rock and water. During the many centuries when virtually all traffic of importance in these parts was sea-borne, it lay in the shelter of an archipelago which invaders found hard to penetrate. Behind Stockholm lay the Mälaren — a vast inland lake system, surrounded by fertile countryside whose waterways gave easy access to such important towns and trading centres as Sigtuna, Uppsala, Strängnäs and Västerås.

And even if the seven centuries since Stockholm was founded seem to have witnessed its total transformation, much of its original character still remains; seems indeed almost eternal.

The best approach to Sweden's capital, if you want to grasp something of its original raison d'être and earliest history, is still by sea. The creeks and sounds may seem narrow; but they open wide enough to admit even very large ships. And then, suddenly, there lies the city, its towers, its church spires, the great façade of the old merchants' houses like a wall facing the water along Skeppsbron quay. If you want to pass on into the Mälaren lakes, then you'll have to go through Slussen — the sluices at the southern end of the Old Town. Or else mount the rapids beneath the Royal Palace, at its northern end.

Even if the Old Town (once known as simply »The Town») used to be a good deal smaller than it is today and the narrows at its either end considerably wider, still Stockholm effectively barred all access to Lake Mälaren. And this was why its fortress, which soon grew out into a whole little town, was founded in the mid-13th century — as an outwork to defend other more important ones. Only after this lock had been prised open could they be approached.

But Stockholm came into existence in an age when petty chieftains were beginning to submit to kings and Sweden was being united into a single king-dom. And so this fortress itself swiftly became the new nation's capital; so that again and again the struggle for the crown was a struggle for the possession of Stockholm. It was a struggle which went on for several centuries, until Mid-summer Eve, 1523, when Gustaf Wasa made his triumphal entry through the now non-existent South Gate. He and his men had wrested the city from the Danish Union King Christian. Since then Stockholm has never once been be-seiged, let alone captured by foreign troops.

Rock and water. Even today Stockholm is still part of its archipelago — as you can best see perhaps, from Fåfängan (»Vanity»), with its 18th-century plea-sure pavilion, on the southern cliffs, opposite Skansen. The whole area has been called »a unique example of a wilderness thrust into the heart of a capital». Se-veral other knolls (Åsöberget, Skinnarviksberget) raise their heads in Söder-malm — the large southern island. An Englishman who visited Stockholm in 1654 found the city lay »as if in the middle of a circle of knolls». And anyone who surveys the city from a sufficient altitude (e.g. from the Kaknäs TV-tower, the roof terrace of the Dagens Nyheter building, or from the air) still gets ex-actly the same impression. An almost unbroken perimeter of forest surrounds it, and more of its inside area consists of water and verdure than anyone strol-ling through its streets would think.

In 1654, the high knolls on Kungsholmen and Norrmalm were still largely uninhabited; and on today's Brunkebergstorg, above today's Gustav Adolfs torg, stood the firewatch tower. Sand and gravel from the Brunkeberg ridge have been used in the construction of almost all Stockholm's older houses. And though layer after layer of gravel has been removed, and the bedrock has everywhere been blasted away, Stockholm is still quite a hilly town. On some of its less accessible knolls surviving old quarters form »historical reserves», de-lightful to stroll through — notably Mariaberget, overlooking Lake Mälaren on the south side, and Åsöberget. Many steep paths lead up to points giving de-lightful views out across the city and its waters. Up to Fjällgatan on Stigberget, for instance; or the Skinnarviksberg heights.

Naturally, Stockholmers have always been fond of their waterways and refer proudly to their city as »The Venice of the North» or the »Queen of Lake Mälaren». This hasn't prevented them from filling them in to make new roads and building sites. Here geology has helped them. Since the last Ice Age, the whole vast slab of granite which is Sweden is still rising steadily, at the rate of about a meter a century. As the land has risen, the broad waters have been reduced to narrow canals and sluices. The great surfaces of gleaming water have dwindled; many isolated lakes and ponds, once a feature of the town, have disappeared. The spectacular Town Hall (Stadshuset) and the Central Station both stand on such artificial foundations. From the south the railway approaches across the floors of dried out lakes (Zinkensdamm, Fatburen). And Birger Jarlsgatan, today one of the largest streets, was once a trickling stream known as Träskrännilen — »the bog spinney».

Even so, Stockholm remains a city of waterways. Innumerable bridges link its islands, islets and peninsulars and join them to the mainland. Under others the Mälaren waters flow out into the slightly saline Archipelago. Stand on the Västerbro bridge a summer's evening, and you'll see how a long stretch of gleaming blue water reaches away westwards into the heart of Central Sweden, while another reaches out eastwards, toward the Archipelago and the Baltic. Once, before the Södertälje Canal was dug (in the 19th century) and the Hammarby channel (in the 20th), Slussen and the North Stream were the only channels joining Lake Mälaren and the sea. For many centuries, too, only a single road linked the town with the counties to north and south, bridging these channels. This made Stockholm a natural junction, through which all travellers by sea or land were obliged to pass. A centre of commerce and a general meeting place.

The earliest town consisted of mere shacks. Its castle, its church and a few stone houses apart, it was made up of single-storey timber houses, strung out along muddy winding narrow streets.

The most stringent regulations and penalties for carelessness did not save Stockholm from again and again being ravaged by fires. After each conflagration, however, more and more timber houses would be replaced by taller ones, built of brick or stone. They went up on the same sites — and this is why the medieval street network has survived, whilst the narrow alleys have become darker and more shadowy than they were to begin with.

Around this little town was built a fortification wall. The first such wall (13th century) ran along the inner sides of what later became Västerlånggatan and Österlånggatan. Subsequent walls, enhanced with gates and towers, ran nearer the water's edge. Outside them, on piles, quays and jetties were built, where long rows of shipping lay tethered.

The town was densely built. A swarm of buildings of every kind sought shelter within the narrow area inside the walls, like a flock of sheep huddling around its shepherds, the church and the castle. The castle was known as Tre Kronor (»Three Crowns» — i.e. the Three Crowns of the united realm of Sweden) and in its immediate neighbourhood no building was allowed. Considerations of defense left a broad gravel slope from the Town Church (Storkyrkan) down to the waterside. Once known as »The Sand», this slope is today's Slottsbacken.

All around, and quite close to the »Town Island», lay extensive land areas. Here were no buildings at all. For centuries they remained pasture land. Yet as early as the 13th century they were known as Norrmalm and Södermalm — »malm» (cognate with the verb »mala» = to grind) actually meaning »sand, gravel, ground up stone». That is, they got their names from the Brunkeberg gravel ridge and its southward extension.

Out there, in the 17th century, the town's wealthier burghers began building summer houses. These came to be known as »malmgårdar» — (gård = farmhouse). Which is why, to the Stockholmer, the word »malm» came to mean a »suburb».

It was thanks to these suburbs that Stockholm could expand. At the same time they were a threat to its existence. Here beseigers lay encamped in wartime, from the high knolls all around aiming their cannon down into the watergirt city. An enemy could turn each such house into a fortress. Yet the crush of people and buildings on the main island was such that all space-consuming, inflammatory or evilsmelling activities had to be carried on outside the town walls; and in the 14th and 15th centuries this led to quite a few buildings — tryworks, rope factories, potteries, tanneries — being erected out there. Even earlier, back in the 13th century, monasteries had been built outside the walls, on what today is called Riddarholmen but was then known as Gråmunkeholmen (»Greyfriars Islet»), and on Norrmalm, both at a safe distance from the city (Klara Monastery).

In troublous times most of these buildings, not excepting the little chapels built on Norrmalm and Södermalm, would be demolished.

By the 16th century the realm and its crown had grown stronger. Now the threat of seige was felt to have receded; and more and more buildings, and of a more permanent nature, came to be erected out there.

At first there was little order among them. The suburbs were a rubbish heap and a wilderness; grazing land and cabbage patches were crossed only by rough paths and tracks leading out through the pasturelands' gates into the countryside.

Some of these paths however, were more frequently trodden than others; for instance, the one from the South Gate to the promontory linking Södermalm with the countryside to the south (Skanstull), and the one from the North Gate to the Uppsala road, across today's Östermalm to the royal barn (which lay where the Nobel Park is now laid out, by Djurgårdsbron Bridge). These paths set the pattern for future developments. They were the town plan of today's down-town Stockholm.

Yet as we walk its streets we see little of the town which stood here between the 13th and early 17th centuries. True, the chancel and north porch of Riddarholm Church reveals bits of its 13th-century façade, elsewhere hidden by later funerary chapels. Beneath Lejonbacken (»Lions' Slope») where the North Bridge approaches the Royal Palace, part of the 13th century curtain wall, built of immense grey granite blocks, is still to be seen in the Palace cellars.

A few 14th, 15th and 16th-century houses are left, though almost all have since been extended or rebuilt. Few still retain the style of the epoch when they were first erected.

Best preserved are the cellars of certain rebuilt houses. The 14th-century cellar of the Blackfriars friary at Södra Benickebrinken, for instance; and that of the Själagårdshus building (Själagårdsgatan 13, 15th cent.)

At the north-west corner of Riddarholmen, one of the towers which once formed part of the 15th and 16th-century town walls can still be seen. Quite incorrectly known as »Birger Jarls Tower», it is certainly not contemporary with Birger Jarl, the 13th-century magnate who, tradition says, founded the city. Dating probably from the 16th century, the tower was extended in the 18th.

Anyone seeking the past in Stockholm will find its earliest traces in the layout of the Old Town (»Gamla Stan») and in the scene around the Great Market (»Stortorget») and the alleys around it; and not least, in the narrow twittens, named after famous sea captains of Gustaf Wasa's day (Skeppar Olof, Peter Fredag, Staffan Sasse), running northwards from Köpmangatan.

Not until the first half of the 17th century did the conditions arise for a new Stockholm.

As so often before, it all began with a great fire. One September night in 1625, some womenfolk in a brewery on Kåkbrinken, near Riddarholmsfjärden, dozed over the fire they'd lit. The place caught fire and a strong west wind swept it into the city, burning down a broad area between the shore and Västerlånggatan.

Out of this catastrophe a new Stockholm arose. And this time not merely new houses on the sites of old, but an entirely new town plan – a new way, for Stockholmers, of building a city.

Many reasons coincided for this departure. King Gustavus Adolphus, »The Lion of the North», protestant hero of the Thirty Years War, wanted a capital worthy of his empire. New military techniques had anyway robbed the ancient town wall of its significance; so it could be pulled down, and new streets – Stora and Lilla Nygatan – laid out in the area laid waste by the fire. A few years later, too, a stately broad quay – Skeppsbron – was built on the island's east side, on freshly filled in land. Ten years more and the city's first governor, Clas Fleming, an energetic and enterprising man, extended the works to include the northern and southern suburbs. It was in his day, (i.e., during the reign of Queen Christina) that a new chequerboard pattern spread out over these outlying and formerly ramshackle districts.

In 1635, the government decided on a plan for Norrmalm. Virtually all its houses must either be demolished or moved elsewhere (timber buildings could be). Ten more years pass and the turn has come to Södermalm; and in the 1640's to today's Östermalm, then known as Ladugårdslandet (»Barn Land», after the royal barns there), and to Kungsholmen, then known as Munklägret (»The Monks' Camp»).

The new chequer pattern was applied to all these new quarters. But in each the pattern was laid out in such a way that the main thoroughfares lay along what until then had been paths.

On Södermalm (»Söder») it is Götgatan — for centuries the only land-route southwards — and Hornsgatan, which provide the backbones of this plan.

For Norrmalm two different patterns are laid out, one on either side of the Brunkeberg Ridge. The watershed between them is Malmskillnadsgatan (»The dividing line between the two suburbs»). Any map shows how West Norrmalm has Drottninggatan (leading to the northern customs barrier and Uppsala) as its axis; whilst the area to the east of Malmskillnadsgatan has Regeringsgatan (leading to Roslagen county and Norrtälje). In Östermalm it is the road from the bridge across the swamp spinney to the Royal Barn (Humlegårdsgatan-Storgatan), and the road to the new bridge (Nybrogatan) across the creek, which are the axes.

On Kungsholmen, an outlying region formerly belonging to the monasteries, no traditional paths could be followed. Kungsholmen is traversed longitudinally by two main streets: Kungsholmsgatan, from the first bridge, and Hantverkargatan, along the craftsmens' and tanners' plots near the Mälaren shore.

Present day down-town Stockholm thus lies spread out in patterns derived from the past. Underneath its modern thoroughfares the medieval paths still lie buried.

Victories in the Thirty Years War brought Sweden — and not least Stockholm — treasure and wealth. Generals and noblemen began building themselves ever statelier palaces, encouraged to do so by a crown which liked to remind the citizens of their duty to build »to the city's enhancement and embellishment, in accordance with whatever design may please His Majesty» — as the instructions read for the Skeppsbron buildings.

Between the 1630's and the end of the century the city developed so swiftly it seems to have sprouted wings. As Stockholm spread out into its north and south suburbs the population exploded. From having about 10,000 inhabitants at the beginning of the century, it had more than 40,000 at its middle. Pride in the city's rebirth and its great size (for that day and age) finds expression in the first major detailed pictures. The prints of Keyser Lastman, Vogel and Sasse were the pioneers. Erik Dahlberg, the most famous of them all, whose prints comprised both views and individual buildings, followed after.

In these prints we see flags fluttering and the sails of many stately ships bellying out before favouring breezes. The city is veritably fenced in by the masts of merchantmen. Already, the first sluice has been built, to facilitate navigation between the Old Town — as we now call it — and Söder. On the steep slope above Slussen (today's Södermalmstorg) boys are flying paper kites, and one is sailing proudly away into the background, high over the knolls of a Kungsholmen as yet populated only with windmills.

It was also on Södermalm, at Mosebacke, that Charles X Gustaf planned to build himself a new palace. But all that came of his plans were the many large private town houses along Götgatan. Here too the Southern City Hall (today the City Museum — Stadsmuseum), was built.

Other notables did their building on the main island, on Riddarholmen and Norrmalm. On Riddarholmen the aristocracy's palaces became particularly numerous: e.g. the Sparre family's house on Birger Jarls torg, the Stenbock's (No. 4), and the Wrangel's (No. 16). Beside what today is Riddarhustorg the nobles and knights raised their stately »House of Chivalry» (Riddarhuset). Next to it the Bonde family built its beautiful palace (today the Supreme Court). New churches were erected or old ones rebuilt. The age's most celebrated architects — Jean de la Vallée and Nikodemus Tessin the Elder, had their hands so full of commissions they hardly had time to execute them all.

So many great new houses totally transformed the town's aspect. Gone was the old muddle of one-storey houses dominated by a few taller ones. A new city, better suited to the demands made by Sweden's so-called Age of Greatness on a capital that should be worthy of itself, had swept them away. Now in the 17th century, a city is built whose aspect hardly changes at all until the mid-19th.

These 17th-century buildings still set their stamp on down-town Stockholm. They grace its shores, dominate and enliven many otherwise uninteresting streets.

At the north-east corner of the Old Town stands the Royal Palace, for centuries a fortress, a massive castle. In the oldest pictures the three crowns which, from the mid-16th century onwards, were to give it its name are not to be seen.

It had been several times extended. All through the 17th century plans for new rebuilds, presented by Jean de la Vallée and the older and younger Nikodemus Tessin, were being discussed. And it was under the latter's supervision that the rebuild of the 1690's had been begun — when the great fire of 1697 interrupted it.

For Sweden and its capital the autumn of 1696 and spring of 1697 were a difficult time. The harvest had failed. Swarms of starving peasants had made their way into town — where no help could be given then. In the spring Charles XI died. Still unburied, he lay in his coffin in the castle.

The fire broke out on May 7, and the dowager queen and the fifteen-year-old Charles XII had to leave the castle in all haste. The dead king's corpse was carried to the Royal Stables on Helgeandsholmen, and thence Riddarholm Church. Meanwhile the fire, leaping from one part of the castle's roofing to another and setting fire to many nearby houses, was spreading at a terrible rate. Finally the keep tower, with its proud symbol the Three Crowns of Sweden, collapsed.

How had it begun? No one ever found out. But with the old Renaissance-style castle conveniently out of the way, the younger Tessin found it much easier to create an entirely new palace. That same year he presented his plans; what remained of the old castle was demolished, and work was begun on a new one. It was an immense project, and it took time; and during the disastrous years of Charles XII's defeats came wholly to a halt. In 1710, a plague carried off 20,000 lives; and by the time Charles XII died (1718) Sweden's Age of Empire was clearly and irrevocably over.

From 1697-1754 the Wrangel Palace, on Riddarholmen, had to serve as the royal abode. And even when the royal family moved into their new palace (1754) it was still far from ready. But the works were going on apace, and as the century drew to a close some order was even beginning to be brought into the palace environs. Today's Gustav Adolfs torg was flanked with two palace-like buildings in identical style: the old Opera, and the so-called Crown Prince's Palace (Ministry for Foreign Affairs). Norrbro, a stately stone bridge, replaced the existing timber one. It was during the 18th century, too, that the quays of the Old Town were paved; first Skeppsbron, then on the Mälaren side.

As a building project, the Royal Palace overshadowed all others. Yet the sluice bridges were rebuilt under the famous engineer Kristoffer Polhem's supervision; the old council chamber on Stortorget was replaced by the new Stock Exchange building (today the seat of the Swedish Academy), and an observatory was established on Brunkeberg. A new church (Adolf Fredrik) was erected, and after great fires Jakob and Katarina churches were both enhanced with their present towers.

It was during the 18th century, too, that Stockholm first began to become an industrial town. Several dockyards were laid out. The Barnängen spinning mills, founded at the end of the previous century, grew into a major establishment. The Rörstrand and Marieberg potteries began turning out porcelain and chinaware. And the Bergsunds foundry came into existence.

Of most of these, little if anything is left today. But what does remain is — by pure chance — concentrated in the eastern part of Söder. One rather well-preserved industrial monument there is Barnängen Manor, with its workshops surrounding the owner's dwelling. On Nytorget square, close by, is »Malongen». Dating from the 1670's when it was a glove factory, the building got its name from an 18th-century proprietor called Madelung. Another textile mill was by Lilla Blecktornet, where one 18th-century building remains. Near Barnängen a dwelling house, once belonging to the dye-works founded there in the late 17th-century, has been preserved. And close to the Hammarbyled Canal, near Danvik bridge, stands Hoving Manor, built in 1770 as a combined dwelling and dyer's mill.

The best approach to Barnängen is by Malmgårdsvägen. Passing Groens »malmgård» (c.1700), you see some extant 18th-century buildings on Malmgårdsvägen's eastern side, leading down to the site of the Winter Customs Barrier. As its name indicates, this was formerly used only in winter, when the Värmdö peasants took a short cut across the ice.

Other parts of Söder that have preserved their 18th-century buildings are the south side of Fjällgatan, the district around Katarina Church, and a cluster of old houses in Ansgariegatan (Wirwachska Malmgården). Still other memories of the 18th-century are to be found in the outskirts. The older houses in Djurgården park; Bellevue; Stora Sjötullen (customs house); Stora Skuggan, near Frescati. Drottningholm Palace was built in the late 17th-century. But its wings, the park and several smaller buildings (e.g. the unique, delightful and still functioning theatre; the Chinese Pavilion, etc.) are from the 18th. So also are several buildings in Haga Park (Gustaf III's pavilion, still fully furnished; the Copper Tents) and the park itself.

The same epoch has left us several charming details to remember it by, all of them the work of Erik Palmstedt, the city architect: the well on Stortorget, Tyska brunn (»The German Well») and the portals of the Serafimer Hospital.

But to all Stockholmers the 18th-century is above all associated with their city's unique poet and song-writer Carl Michael Bellman (1740-1795). Who ever described its life so vividly as he? Bellman's whole amazing opus is a kind of guided tour of 18th Stockholm and of what, in his day, were its surroundings.

One of his best friends was the great sculptor Johan Tobias Sergel (1740-1814). Sergel's statue of Gustaf III, that great patron of the arts, stands on Skeppsbron. Another man of genius encouraged by the king was the painter Elias Martin (1739-1818). In his soft airy drawings and entrancing watercolours he loved above all to depict the urban scene from the town's various shores. From Mosebacke Martin also painted (in oils) an immense panorama of the »classic» Stockholm which was so long to remain unchanged and which Strindberg describes in the introduction to his novel »The Red Room» (1879).

The 19th-century meant an end to the age of monumental buildings, aristocratic palaces and great merchants' houses. Around the Royal Palace, cleaning up operations still continue. The Strömparterr, a little tongue of land jutting out into the rapids of the North Stream, is designed; and to hide the ugly Royal Stables the North Bridge is enhanced with a long bazaar along its western parapet, not demolished until the Riksdag (parliament) building was erected.

Blasieholmen, facing the Palace, was still a muddle of shacks, woodyards, a sugar mill, slaughter houses, etc. In 1822 most of this disappeared in a fire. And so, in 1825, did the palace known as »Makalös» (Nonpareil). Once built by the 17th-century magnate Magnus Gabriel de la Gardie, it stood at the south end of Kungsträdgården. In its last years it was used as an arsenal (whence Arsenalsgatan) and a theatre. And it was during a performance, one November evening in 1825, it went up in flames.

These fires cleared a good deal of space and enabled something more elegant to be made of the Palace environs. Once Kungsträdgården (»The King's Garden») had been a baroque garden. But Karl XIV Johan (Marshal Bernadotte, as was) cut down its trees, turned it into a sand-strewn parade ground, and put up a statue of Karl XIII, the last Wasa king, in the middle.

It is perhaps typical that the speciality of the chief early 19th-century architect, Fredrik Blom, was building movable timber houses. Rosendal however, the loveliest of these, is still where it was first erected in Djurgården. Other Blom creations are the church on Skeppsholmen, the castle on Kastellholmen, and the Post Office in Lilla Nygatan.

During the troubled years of the Napoleonic wars various military establishments came into existence. Blom erected barracks on Skeppsholmen and in Östermalm's Storgatan (today the Office of National Antiquities). C.C. Gjörwell was the architect for the Garrison Hospital (today the County Council offices) in Hantverkargatan, Kungsholmen.

These efforts apart, the city did not change much in the century's first decades. It was, and remained, a poor and very dirty town. Both for its beauty and its filth people compared it with Constantinople. The death-rate was quite extraordinary — twice as high as for the countryside. Enormous heaps of rubbish and sewage — known as the flies' meeting places — lay rotting along the town's shores; and cholera epidemics were frequent. The cobbled streets made the going hard — not until the mid-19th century were any of them paved with granite. Most local traffic therefore went by water. The ferries were rowed by »madams», famed for their foul language. Only in the 1830's did they begin to meet with competition from paddleboats, hand-powered by peasant girls from Dalarna.

But though early 19th-century Stockholm seems to have gone to sleep, actually it is on the verge of a new dawn.

Now all sorts of things begin to happen. For Sweden the century's latter half was the age of great population migrations. People flocked from the countryside and agriculture into town, to industry. Within fifty years Stockholm grows from being a city of just under 100,000 inhabitants to one of over 300,000. Many of these migrants left Sweden altogether; quitting a country unable to support its offspring, they sought a new life in USA. During the 1880's, an average of 40,000 Swedes were emigrating every year. Within a decade the country lost a tenth of its population.

But around 1860 there are many signs of a new age and a new city.

In 1864 Stockholm gets a municipal council. At the same time as local government is introduced, all the old restrictions on trades and professions are swept away. New industries and enterprises become possible. In 1865, the first step is taken toward modern democratic government. A two-chamber parliament replaces the old Four Estates of the Realm.

In the spheres of technology and hygiene, too, much is happening. Steam-power is being ever more widely used. The innumerable windmills on the surrounding heights disappear in favour of »Steam mills». Now the oarswomen have to compete with little steam sloops. Sailing schooners are outstripped by steamboats. In 1860, the steam railway links Stockholm with Södertälje. And the seventies see the first horse-drawn trams.

In 1861 the city gets its first piped water supply. A few years later the first sewage pipes are laid down. At last, it was said, filth — that age-old tyrant — had been overthrown! Statistics show how the town's health improved. The public health graph runs parallel with those for the number of water and sewage pipes laid down.

The enormous immigration from the countryside, creating an acute shortage of dwellings, gave rise to the social abuse known as the »lodging system» — but also to numerous new buildings, many of them huge tenements.

Industries grow, both in size and number. Many major factories are established in what today is down-town Stockholm: Karlsvik, Bolinders and Separator on Kungsholmen, Atlas in the »Wasa Town», Ludwigsberg on Söder, and many others. The new railways are also attracting industries, and around 1870 the first modern suburban areas (Sundbyberg and Liljeholmen) come into being.

Such swift growth demanded not only new houses, but also new streets, new street plans. One of the city council's first tasks had been to set up a committee to present proposals. Clearly inspired by Hausmann's plans for Napoleon III's Paris, these 1866 plans also featured broad boulevards. Defying the old chequerboard pattern, they were to meet at »étoiles».

These plans may have seemed altogether too grandiose for the little Stockholm of those days, with its small amount of street traffic. Yet they were rather closely implemented. Even today, Albert Lindhagen's boulevards — Strandvägen, Narvavägen, Valhallavägen, Birger Jarlsgatan, Odengatan, Kungsgatan, Sveavägen, Norr Mälarstrand, Ringvägen — still form the city's main thoroughfares. But only one »étoile» was realised: Karlaplan.

One purpose of the Lindhagen plan was to »let in air and light» and thus make Stockholm a healthier city. So naturally it allowed for plenty of large parks, for which it left most of the less accesible rocky areas free.

This long-term plan was to be implemented from the perimeter inwards. It was easier to make a start in the less thickly populated outer areas, with their one or two-storey mostly timber houses. Down-town, it sufficed to ban the erection of any new building that did not accord with the plan.

The latter 19th century saw great improvements in Sweden's and her capital's communications with other countries. It introduced new ideas and such novel building materials as panelling, woodblock flooring and lath ceilings. At first these novelties — iron girders and piping, etc. — were mostly imported from Britain; then from Belgium and Germany. Afterwards Sweden began manufacturing her own.

Much of the building work was purely speculative, so there were periods when too much accommodation was available and others with too little. There were huge profits and terrible financial crashes. But there were also many buildings of another character, and of these many still remain: Konradsberg Hospital (1860), the Technical College in Drottninggatan (1863), Berns Restaurant (1863), the National Museum, containing Sweden's art collections (1866), the Synagogue in Wahrendorffsgatan (1870), the Central Station (1871), the Grand Hotel (1874), Bredablick (1876), the Royal Library (1877), the Östermalm indoor market (1888), Johannes Church (1890), the Royal Stables in Väpnargatan (1893), and the Hallwylska Palace in Hamngatan (1899) are all typical of that era.

The 1890's saw several monumental buildings put in hand. The new Opera, on Gustav Adolfs torg, was built between 1891 and 1898 (architect: A. Anderberg). In 1897, the new »State Buildings» (Parliament House and the Riksbank; architect, Aron Johansson) were begun on Helgeandsholmen, but only after furious protests and discussions. The huge buildings were felt to be excessive for the little islet, the more so as they hid the point of confluence between the waters of lake Mälaren and of the Archipelago.

Another building begun in the 1890's was the Nordiska Museet, in Djurgården (architect: J.G. Clason). Arthur Hazelius had founded the world's first open-air museum up on Skansen, and he wanted the indoor section to consist of wholly Swedish materials, thus making it »the first monumental building of Swedish national character in modern times». The Nordic Museum came to set the style for many of the town's early 20th-century buildings.

It was also in the 1890's that the first real suburban housing estates grew up. The 1870's and 1880's have already seen one earlier suburban villa experiment — the so called Villa Town, north of Humlegården. But this lay inside the city boundaries. In the 1890's people began reaching further afield. Djursholm and Saltsjöbaden come into being, both attractive areas for the wealthy, and linked with the centre of town by narrow-gauge electric railways.

The great Stockholm 1897 Exhibition of Arts and Industries, in Djurgården, was a rather way-out blend of patriotic enthusiasm (Royal Jubilee celebrations, the rebuilding of »Old Stockholm») and oriental pipe-dreams (minarets and onion-shaped cupolas). Ferdinand Boberg, the Exhibition's architect, was to set his style — gentle Art Noveau curves and sumptuous ornament — on much of the turn-of-the century Stockholm. Among Boberg's surviving buildings are the water tower on Mosebacke, Rosenbad beside The Stream, the Central Post Office in Vasagatan, Prince Eugen's Waldemarsudde, and the Thielska Gallery (both in Djurgården), and NK, the great department store in Hamngatan.

But as the 20th-century begins, other architects are trying to achieve a new style of building, based on earlier Swedish architectural traditions. Oddly, hand-made brick again becomes »modern» and is widely used, at the very moment when building materials are just beginning to become thoroughly industrialized.

Typical representatives of this style are Carl Westman's Council House (1910-1916), Torben Grut's Stadium (1912) and — to crown it all — Ragnar Östberg's Town Hall, built 1912-1923 and inaugurated on the 400th anniversary of Gustav Wasa's entry into Stockholm on midsummer eve 1523. Two new churches also witness to the same style of architectural thinking: Engelbrektskyrkan (1914, L.I. Wahlman) and Högalidskyrkan (1923, Ivar Tengbom).

Another phenomenon typical of that age was the home ownership dream, with its »little plot of land». It was realized in many variants, tuned to the dreamer's financial resources. In 1906, Anna Lindhagen, daughter of town-planner Lindhagen, introduced the allotment movement into Stockholm. And even today the city has a number of well-tended allotment colonies, some even in its central districts (Barnängen, Eriksdal). It is also around the turn of the century that many new housing estates and summer cottage areas begin to sprout up around the town, at first mostly as a fruit of private initiative. Some of these were pure speculations in the housing shortage (e.g. Årstadal on Liljeholmen); others were allowed to spring up almost unrestrictedly. This gave rise to suburban areas where the joys of fancy carpentry seem to have been allowed to run riot, with the oddest results (e.g. at Hagalund, now demolished). True, some attempts at social building were aimed simply at providing good quality housing, the best results being those of an organization called Hem på Landet, (»Home in the Country»), which built Duvbo and Solhem.

But in 1904 the city authorities intervened by buying up a number of large farms and estates, among others Enskede manor, Ulvsunda and Åkeshov. In 1908, a town plan was drawn up for Enskede. The city retained the land but divided it up into building plots, which it sold off leasehold. The whole project was publicly supervised.

Outside the old customs barriers it was mainly single-family houses that were being built. A whole network of such suburbs grew around the city. In some the road network, drainage, water supply and streetlighting long remained very primitive. In some cases they improved after the city had incorporated Brännkyrka in 1913 and Bromma in 1916.

The First World War and the years immediately following put a brake on developments. Yet some new additions were made. Somewhat in protest at earlier stylistic deliriums and poor quality building materials, several rather unified and elegant districts were created: e.g. Rödaberg (1914-1925) and Helgalund (1913-1920). By the mid-twenties Stockholm's two tallest buildings of the time were finished: the North and South Towers on either side of Kungsgatan, then the main shopping street.

Now simplification of form and functional building styles became the watchwords. E.G. Asplund's City Library (in Sveavägen) was an early attempt along these lines that had aroused much comment. Many an indignant Stockholmer had likened it to a »beer can standing on a crate». Later, Asplund became the architect of the 1930 Stockholm Exhibition, which presented the new style in many variants, thus further fanning the flames of discussion. The planned apartment blocks of Kungsklippan, Gärdet and part of Norr Mälarstrand can all be seen as early fruits of these new functionalist ideas.

The later twenties and thirties saw great changes beginning to be planned.

Many factories that took up too much space in the central areas were moved out (Atlas 1925, Rörstrand 1926, Bergsund 1929, Bolinders 1932, to mention only four of the largest). After which the ground they had occupied was used for housing. New industrial areas sprung up outside the old customs barriers (Södra Hammarby Harbour, Ulvsunda Industrial Estate). The Free Harbour was completed in 1926; the Hammarby Canal in 1929; and Bromma Airport in 1936.

It is also now that the big bridges begin to be built. Pontoon bridges, themselves earlier having supplanted floating bridges, begin (but at first only cautiously) to yield to soaring spans. The Liljeholm Bridge is ready in 1928; the railway bridge over Årstaviken the year after. In 1934, the Traneberg Bridge's proud span is inaugurated; and the following year the iron-framed Västerbron. The 1930's see the total transformation of Slussen into a highly functionalistic clover-leaf switchway system.

In 1930, the planners realise that there will soon be no room for further developments inside the town that had once been bounded by customs barriers. Apartment blocks must start encroaching on the villa suburbs. Plans were adopted for Traneberg and part of what today is Hammarbyhöjden. Work began there in the mid-thirties, some of the buildings being finished before the outbreak of World War II.

In the post-war years, the rush of apartment houses really begins to spread out over what hitherto had been fields and forests, necessitating a whole new communications network. Trains and busses no longer suffice and public transport got stuck in traffic jams.

Until 1950 a tunnel, blasted through the bedrock southwards from Slussen in the thirties, was only used by trams. As early as 1941, however, it had been decided to give the city an underground railway system. Work began in the late forties — wartime paucity of road traffic made it easier to open up long stretches of thoroughfare (Sankt Eriksgatan, Odengatan, Sveavägen) for this purpose.

Even so, many large buildings had to be demolished; and a new town plan for much of Norrmalm, particularly around Klara Church and Hötorget, now became possible. During the fifties, sixties and well into the seventies much of down-town Stockholm consisted mainly of vast holes — huge cavities, out of which a new City Centre, dominated by the five skyscrapers on Sveavägen and Hötorget, was gradually coming into being. Hamngatan's steep slope disappeared, to make room for the new Klaraberg trafficway. Brunkebergstorg has been totally transformed. The Riksdag (parliament) has moved into the huge glass-façaded House of Culture. Numerous banks and large commercial buildings cluster around Edvin Öhrström's 37-meter vertical crystal »exclamation mark in glass and steel» in the centre of Sergels torg.

The underground/subway (»Tunnelbanan») between Kungsgatan and Vällingby was inaugurated even while these works were still going on (1952); likewise, in 1957, the Kungsgatan-Slussen link. Since then new sections have been added, linking the south-western and north-eastern suburbs. Also and most recently, the line out to Järvafältet. These surface lines link the city with the new suburbs which have been proliferating so swiftly ever since the 1940's.

The first suburb where an attempt was made to create a major shopping centre was Årsta. Compared with the satellite towns of Vällingby (1952-1956), Farsta (1960-1961), Skärholmen (1966-1968) and Kista (1970's), Årsta Centre, built by Erik and Tore Ahlsén between 1946 and 1953, seems modest enough, even idyllic.

Present day Stockholm is a compact centre around which Greater Stockholm, consisting of 20 independent municipalities, spreads out far and wide. To the visitor these municipalities' exact boundaries may be of no interest. To the people who live in them they are important. About half a Swede's income tax goes to the municipality (»kommun») where he lives; and the rate can vary considerably on either side of an otherwise invisible boundary.

That Greater Stockholm comprises some 20 Skogsvägs, 19 Ringvägs, 11 Fasanvägs, etc., can be a troublesome discovery. But all public transport is coordinated by the county council.

Some of Greater Stockholm's outlying communities are older than Stockholm itself. Long before Stockholm was born or thought of, both Birka (in Ekerö municipality) and Sigtuna were once capitals of the Svea Kingdom. And large parts of today's Stockholm formerly formed part of Solna. Other municipalities have sprung up in what not long ago was almost unpopulated countryside. Others, again, e.g. Vaxholm and Värmdö, are also »summer towns», their shores lined with Stockholmers' summer houses.

It seems likely that Greater Stockholm will tend to fuse into a single city, each district hopefully retaining as much as possible of its own character, practical problems — e.g. communications — meanwhile being solved to universal satisfaction.

Stockholm, a city of rocks and waterways, retains many features and memories from its past. Yet it lives very intensely in the present and is working purposively toward its future. Past, present and future must blend. History must be preserved and the present lived, both for the future. At the same time, Stockholm must never be allowed to become just a museum. It must be a home, at once practical, safe and delightful, for the million or so people who live there.

The Old Town

Together with Riddarholmen and Helgeandsholmen, the Old Town — or The Town between the Bridges — is Stockholm's kernel and origin. The central point in this ancient city, which began to grow up in the 13th century close to the royal castle known as »Three Crowns», was Stortorget, the Great Market. Its Council House stood on the site of the Old Stock Exchange building of today, where the Swedish Academy has its seat. All the town's three main streets (Köpmangatan, Svartmangatan and Skomakargatan) led off from Stortorget. Mediaeval streets had to be eight ells (just under 5 m.) wide; but lanes and alleys could be extremely narrow. Outside stood the town walls; and beyond them two roads skirted the shore. In due course these roads were destined to become Västerlånggatan and Österlånggatan. The original island, that is to say, was a good deal smaller than what it is today.

Indeed, it was soon found to be altogether too cramped. Houses began to spring up on accretions of rubbish and land, added as a result of the rising land-level. In this way the two roads became main streets, houses of brick and stone replaced the timber ones; and the entrances to lanes were vaulted over.

Even today much survives of the mediaeval street network. The Old Town's charming façades conceals many a relic of mediaeval buildings, incorporated in their successors. »A historic document of irreplaceable value, even by international standards», the Old Town is an integral part of the modern living city.

Helgeandsholmen (»The Island of the Holy Spirit») gets its name from the mediaeval hospital and poor house which once stood on it. For a long while the islet afterwards served as a kind of royal back yard, with stables and housing for officials. Around the turn of the present century massive — some said altogether too massive — Parliament and State Bank buildings were erected on it.

At the end of the 13th century grey friars built a friary and church (today's Riddarholmskyrkan) on Riddarholmen, whose mediaeval name was to be Greyfriars Island. Its present appellation (»Knigths' Island») dates from the 17th century, when many noble families built palaces on it.

Norrström (»The North Stream») has been called »one of this world's early morning adventures»; and certainly for a large city to have rapids foaming through its centre is highly unusual.
Left: A fisherman mends his net on the jetty just below Strömgatan — even today there are a few game fish to be caught in »The Stream». In the background, the Royal Palace, the Strömparterre promontory, and the old Parliament building.

Today Västerlånggatan is a lively shopping thoroughfare; a favourite traffic-free precinct, it is linking up the city's northern and southern sides.

The Changing of the Guard. The blue of the guardsmen's uniforms dates from the days of Charles XII; the »Pickelhaube» helmets from Oscarian (pre-1914) days.

The oldest parts of Stockholm, seen from the tower of the City Hall. Left: the Royal Palace and Storkyrkan (cathedral). In front of them, Riddarhuset (»House of Nobles») with its twin baroque pavilions. Centre: the German Church and Riddarholmen islet, with Riddarholm Church to the right. Furthest right: Slussen and Södermalm, with Katarina Church and the Mosebacke watertower jutting up above the skyline.

Corner of Skeppar Olofs gränd and Trädgårdsgatan. The latter is named after a royal garden which once flourished here. The corner house, rebuilt in the 18th century, comprises remains of a mediaeval building.

The beautiful »Rose Door» in Staffan Sasses gränd seems to have been constructed out of sections of an open fireplace from some now vanished dwelling.

Gåsgränd (»Goose Alley») seen from the arch at its entrance from VäsΤerlånggatan, looking down towards Riddarfjärden, the shore of Lake Mälaren. On the left, just where the tiny »Goose Square» opens out, can be glimpsed the so-called cannonball doorway (17th c.).

Sunset almost blends the towers of Riddarholm Church with that of the City Hall. In the foreground, Skeppsbron Quay, with Räntmästarhuset and Räntmästartrappan steps, both named after the royal accountant Cronberg, who was appointed »räntmästare» in 1653.

Södermalm

For a long while »Söder» — the island to the south of the Old Town — was mainly pastureland. Certain troublesome activities were also situated there. Likewise evil-smelling tryworks and seal fisheries, exiled to Stadsgården, potteries (always a fire risk) and space-demanding ropeworks. Also the gallows. Until the 1630's it stood on Stigberget, but was then moved out to Skanstull.

Up to 1570 both Norrmalm and Södermalm were outlying areas, administratively subordinate to the city. A charter of that year incorporated them, stipulating that their inhabitants »hereafter shall be counted among the population of the city of Stockholm».

The earliest buildings would seem to have grown up close to the South Gate, i.e., near present-day Slussen. In the 1640's a street plan was drawn up for Södermalm; and thereafter its population grew apace, mainly along Götgatan, where several noble palaces were built. Close to the Danvik charitable institution and Hammarby Lake (under today's Danvik Bridge) an early suburb sprang up.

It was a long while before Södermalm became at all easy of access. Its heights could only be reached by steep slopes and rickety flights of steps. Much remained countryside, or at best outskirts. Other parts were occupied by industries and the squalid habitations of the poor. At the same time »malmgårdar» — well-to-do summer residences — and their gardens sprang up out here, »far out in the country». Here idyll and poverty existed cheek by jowl. Many of the older buildings, being so difficult to access, were allowed to remain, since it was unprofitable to demolish and replace them. And this is why present-day Söder has retained more such buildings, and is more of a cultural museum, than any other part of Stockholm, the Old Town always excepted.

Söder's high knolls offer splendid views over the city and its waters.

Mariaberget, the knoll overlooking the south shore of Lake Mä-laren, has been piously restored and preserved. Many of its buildings are 18th-century. Others, among them the most characteristic, date from any time up to the end of the last century. The Laurin House, for instance, with its soaring towers; and the Maria Lift, with its numerous little turrets.

Maria Steps, here seen from Pryss-gränd, leads up to Tavastgatan and Brännkyrkagatan, and so on in the direction of Hornsgatan. They offer a short cut to the heights overlooking Lake Mälaren.

Pryssgränd's charming little 18th-century houses with their saddle-back roofs and attic windows form a sensuous curve down this cobbled street on Mariaberget. Two large windmills used to stand nearby.

Quite a few old wooden houses can still be found clinging to Söder's knolls and heights. Here is one on Åsöberget, near Kvastmakare (»Broom-maker») Steps. Behind the tree we glimpse Fåfängan (»Vanity»), an old lookout fort where there is a café. Furthest to the left can be seen Masthamnen's cranes and an early 19th-century country house. The blue suburban train is speeding on its way along the Saltsjöbaden line.

Internally, Lotsgatan's renovated cottages are fully modernized. What was once a gravelled lane has been paved with cobblestones.

Tegelvikshamnen, the terminal for ferries to Finland and Åland. Ersta Cliff stands up sharply above Stadsgården quay. In the background: The Old Town, fronted by Skeppsbron quay, once thronged with sailing ships.

Heleneborgsgatan and Högalid Church (completed in 1923), seen from Långholmen. In the foreground, the roof of Heleneborg, an 18th-century manor house.

Back in the 1930's a gardener called Josef Johansson planted a magnolia tree near a market garden dating back to the 17th century and a country house from the 18th. The tree was a memorial to Elsa Borg, a pioneer of social work among children and young people out here in the 1870's. The local people assemble annually to celebrate the magnolia tree's flowering. The statue of Elsa Borg and one of her protégés is by Astri Taube. In the background, Sofia Church (completed 1906).

Kungsholmen

In the 1640's Queen Christina donated Kungsholmen island to the city. Prior to the Reformation it had been known as Munklägret and had belonged to the Franciscans. But now more room was needed for craftsmen and industries; so the authorities attracted people out to Kungsholmen by the offer of a ten-year tax-free existence. First to be exploited were the areas between Hantverkargatan and the northern shore of Lake Mälaren, where several large tanneries were established. In the interior some fine big gardens were laid out, but for a long while the western outskirts remained »unspoiled countryside», with manor houses, farms and summer residences.

But gradually Kungsholmen's character changed. Craftsmen gave place to industries; also to many hospitals. Close to Hantverkargatan (on the site of the old Royal Mint) Samuel Owen built the first Swedish steamboats. The city's first steam-powered mill, too, stood on reclaimed land where the Town Hall now stands. The Bolinder and Separator companies had their factories at Kungsklippan and in Fleminggatan. Around Marieberg and Rålambshov other industries sprang up. Kungsholmen's first major hospital was the Serafimer Hospital (1750's). From the mid-19th century up to the 1930's Kungsholmen was a working class district, sometimes known as »Starvation Island».

Its transformation from an industrial suburb into part of down-town Stockholm has been swift. Norr Mälarstrand was laid out along the shore, on the sites of the earlier tanneries; and almost everywhere industries were ousted by residential and office blocks. Indeed, modern Stockholm is administered from Kungsholmen. The Council House, the police headquarters, Law Courts etc., all stand on sites of what once were large market gardens.

Only a single bridge joined Kungsholmen to the rest of the city; and people complained. Today there are so many bridges – Västerbron, Tranebergsbron, the Essinge bridges – that Kungsholmen is in danger of being swamped by through traffic.

Ragnar Östberg's sumptuous Town Hall (inaugurated 1923) is never more imposing than when seen from Riddarholmen at sunset.

Norr Mälarstrand, developed successively between 1900 and the 1930's along Lake Mälaren's northern shore, is Kungsholmen's finest thoroughfare. It has been called »Stockholm's Manhattan». Right centre: the Town Hall.

A view of the new — and perhaps rather overwhelming — office blocks on Marieberg, seen from the Rålambshov Park, Norr Mälarstrand.

In 1848-1850 the Royal Mint moved into buildings in Hantverkargatan which until then had been Samuel Owen's factory and
home, where he had built his steamboats. The gateway, designed by Erik Palmstedt in 1773, came into existence at a time
when the whole district was owned by a wealthy furrier. The
Mint is no longer in Stockholm.

In the early 1960's new buildings were erected on Marieberg for the main daily papers Dagens Nyheter-Expressen and Svenska Dagbladet, which had moved out from the Klara district. Proximity to the Central Station, once essential, was no longer so.

Norrmalm

Even before Stockholm came into being, Norrmalm had probably been of some importance. A prehistoric village called Väsby is thought to have stood more or less on the site of the new City Centre and to have gradually been transformed into a dairy farm and a stud, owned by Klara Monastery. Founded in the 1280's, the latter had dominated this district until dissolved in 1527 at the Reformation.

In the mid-15th century the Crown purchased much land out here, and a royal garden — »Kungsträdgården» — came into being. But even though the population grew so swiftly during the 16th century that in 1602 Norrmalm was given its own charter and separated from the rest of the city, it long remained largely uninhabited and its independence was short-lived. In 1635, Queen Christina's regency decided that it should again become part of the capital; and that same year a street plan was drawn up, which, facilitated by the great fire of 1640, swept away virtually all the older buildings. Subsequently there have been major modifications, particularly to the Klara district, where there was another great fire in 1751. The Cenral Station (1872) led to Klara's transformation into a modern urban area, and in the 1940's many of its older houses began to be demolished to make way for Sergel's torg and the new City Centre.

Blasieholmen, Skeppsholmen and Kastellholmen are also regarded as belonging to Norrmalm. Of these islets, the first originally consisted of two islets, separated from the town by rapids. All four were mainly naval establishments. In the 1630's and 1640's the naval base moved over to Skeppsholmen. Three centuries later, in the 1950's Skeppsholmen and Kastellholmen were converted to civilian uses.

Sergels torg, named after the great 18th-century sculptor Tobias Sergel, who had his studio here, owes its existence mainly to the convulsive transformation of down-town Stockholm as a result of the development of the Underground (Subway — »Tunnelbanan»). The five skyscrapers which dominate the City Centre and Sveavägen went up in 1952-1956. In 1974 the House of Culture, with its vast glass façade, was inaugurated. Opposite, in the middle of a basin and fountains stands Edvin Öhrström's pillar of glass, illumined from within.

»Gallerian», Stockholm's latest shopping arcade, runs between Hamngatan and the Kungsträdgården underground station and Jakobsgatan.

The rather shabby older houses that still remain tend to attract porn and one-arm bandit shops, for instance here in Gamla Brogatan. But also boutiques where the younger generation buys its clothes.

Unfortunately, Sergels torg has become a gathering place for drug addicts and drifters. The diligent hurry past. Appealing equally to both, Maria Johansson sits in the middle of it all, singing her revivalist religious songs.

The market hall which once stood on Hötorget (»The Haymarket») has gone underground; but the market itself still flourishes. Its history goes back to the 17th century.

Even in the Middle Ages a royal garden occupied the site of today's Kungstädgården. Gradually, after being mainly a kitchen garden, it became a pleasure park. In the 1820's its trees and hedges were swept away to make room for a parade ground; and King Karl XIV Johan put up a statue to Karl XIII, the last Vasa king. In the late 19th century the park was taken over by the city authorities. Today it is a favourite spot with Stockholmers, both in summer and winter.

Moored permanently at the shore of Skeppsholmen lies the old full-rigged ship »af Chapman». Named after a famous 18th-century Swedish ship-builder, she was built in Britain in 1888, sailed first as the »Dunboyn», then as the »C.D. Kennedy». In 1923, she was bought by the Swedish state to train seamen, and is today the Swedish Touring Club's floating youth hostel. In the background: the Katarina district and its church.

A controversial modernistic sculpture, called »Paradise», stands at the entrance to Skeppsholmen, once Stockholm's naval base.

61

The Vasa Town

The name dates only from the late 1880's, presumably as a result of a plan, then drawn up, to extend Vasagatan northwards from Norra Bantorget. Until then »Vasastan» had always been regarded simply as part of Norrmalm.

Here an extensive residential district sprang up to the south of Odengatan, mostly between 1900 and 1910, when the Rörstrand porcelain factory had begun to provide its employees with better housing.

Previously all this area had been a rural suburb, with a few large houses, such as Rörstrand Castle (dating from the 1630's) which today forms part of the Filadelfia Church, and Bellevue (1750's). Also several spas and inns. Norrmalms Hälsobrunn (also known as »surbrunnen» on account of its acidulous waters) was discovered in the late 17th century.

Here several important highways ran out into the countryside: to Roslagen, to Uppsala (a continuation of Drottninggatan) and to Karlberg (a road long known as Karlbergs allé).

In 1726, a porcelain factory was founded at Rörstrand; and in 1874 the Atlas Company, constructors of railroads and bridges, began industrial operations here. Around 1925 both these firms moved out from Stockholm, making room for new residential blocks. Thanks not least to the St. Erik Bridge (opened in 1906) this suburb, where as late as 1839 wolves had prowled, had become part of down-town Stockholm.

Odenplan, an important traffic and public transport junction.

The Rödaberg district, built 1914-1925 (architect: Per Olof Hallman) is quiet and diffident, and has real uniformity of character. Hallman wanted people to feel at home even out of doors; and it was his idea to run smaller streets between the major thoroughfares.

Part of the Vasa Town grew up in the grounds of Rörstrand castle, afterwards owned by the porcelain works. Many of its houses were built by Dorph and Höög, a firm of architects; and some 240 of these still stand. Those shown in the photo (Rörstrandsgatan 56-46, a block known as »The Volunteer») form a kind of bastion to the northwest, in the direction of Solna. Immediatly below runs the main railway line to the north of Sweden.

67

Östermalm

Until well into the 19th century Östermalm was separated from Norrmalm by a stream which ran from »The Bog» (today's Eriksbergsplan) to Nybroviken. It was known as »The Rill», and flowed down more or less today's Birger Jarlsgatan.

Until 1885 Östermalm was known as Ladugårdslandet, (»The Barnland»). And indeed, up to about 1670 royal barns and cowsheds had stood there; even later it remained something of a royal larder. In 1619, a royal hop garden (»Humlegården») was laid out. And still today the Royal bakery is Östermalm's oldest building. Royal stables were erected in Väpnargatan as late as 1891.

In 1639 it had been decided to let the city invade Ladugårdslandet. But seafaring folk were given priority; already many seamen, gunners and fireworkmakers were living around what today is Artillerigatan. The shoreline was mostly owned by the wealthy.

Even as late as 1850 the whole district was very much of a slum. But in the following decades many of its knolls and rocks were blasted away to make room for long straight streets – the so-called »Esplanade system». Since the district had now become highly respectable, its new occupants wanted to change its name, which had unpleasant associations. After some demur the City Council agreed to it being rechristened Östermalm.

Since Östermalm verges on Gärdet common – always the city's parade and drill ground – it also included many barracks. Today most have been converted to civilian purposes.

Humlegårdsgatan-Storgatan, once a track leading out to the royal cowsheds and, until Strandvägen was built, to Djurgården park, has always been Östermalm's main street. Strandvägen, commenced in 1862, was not inaugurated until 1897, the year of the Great Stockholm Exhibition.

Begun in the 1860's, Strandvägen was opened to traffic in 1897. No. 35 (1890-1892, architect J. Laurentz) has one of the street's typical elaborate doorways.

Östermalm's indoor market (1885-1889, architects I.G. Clason and K. Sahlin) is still largely unchanged, both inside and out. Its massive cast iron-work was made at Motala; and it also retains its old carved wooden super-structure.

Jungfrugatan leads to Storgatan and to Hedvig Eleonora Church. Begun in 1669, work on the church soon came to a halt for lack of funds, and was not resumed until 1725, to fresh designs by G.J. Adelcrantz. Though consecrated in 1737, its dome only dates from the 1860's.
Jungfrugatan (»Virgin Street») is called after Sigrid Banér, a noblewoman who once owned mills and a garden here in the 17th century.

The accesses to Tysta Gatan (»The Silent Street», c. 1915) were
made intentionally narrow, to exclude noise from the adjoining
major thoroughfares.

Every spring and autumn the King's sheep pass through the city streets during the night, on their way from Åkeshov out to Ladugårdslandet and Gärdet, where they will graze all summer, until they return in the autumn. Here they are seen on Valhalla-vägen.

Djurgården

Today the name refers only to the part of what once was a far-flung royal hunting park known as Southern Djurgården. The northern parts have been divided up between Ladugårdslandet, Hjorthagen and Brunnsviken (with Frescati and the University).

It was King Johan III who first fenced in Djurgården, in the late 1570's. Queen Christina opened parts of it to the public; and by the latter half of the 18th century the part nearest to the town had gradually become a popular pleasure resort.

In 1829 the royal deer were moved to a smaller enclosure, today's Hjorthagen, where they remained until 1890, when they had to move again, this time to Gripsholm park.

The quaint old district known as the Djurgården Town, with its cobbled streets and old houses, was first inhabited in the 1660's by sick and retired seamen.

Its earliest cottages have disappeared, and their sites are occupied by houses of later date. Western Djurgården has always been associated with shipyards, both naval (Galärvarvet) and commercial. In the 1970's the former area has been turned into a park; but its old wall and seamen's church still stand.

Even today there are still a few very exclusive houses out in Djurgården; their occupants are tenants of the Crown. But mostly Djurgården has become Stockholm's Hyde Park. It has a fairground (Tivoli), several restaurants and museums, of which the largest is Skansen. The first outdoor cultural museum in the world, Skansen was the creation of Arthur Hazelius (1901). The Nordic Museum, the Wasa Museum, housing the salvaged 17th-century flagship »Wasa», and Waldemarsudde, formerly the residence of the painter Prince Eugen, are all open to the public. Rosendal, a charming little pavilion, contains relics from the days of Karl XIV Johan, founder of the present dynasty.

Autumn scene on the banks of the Djurgårdsbrunn Canal. An earlier waterway was blocked up in the 17th century. The present canal was dug in the 1830's.

Djurgården was once surrounded by a high fence and could only be entered through one or another of its few gates. Of these the most important was the »Pleasure Pavilion Gate«, named after a now vanished royal pavilion; or the Blue Gate, near which once stood a famous inn of the same name. The present gateway dates from 1849, but has twice been moved: first to the Nobel Park and then to Frescati. In 1967 it was brought back to its original site. This imposing villa stands on the site of the old inn, which burnt down in 1869. Originally the home of a cork manufacturer and dating from the 1870's, it was rebuilt 1899-1900. Since 1941 it has been used by the Institute for Nordic Ethnography.

Stora Sjötullen (»The Great Sea Customs»), on Blockhusudden promontory, was built in 1727 from plans by J.E. Carlberg and in the 1750's it was the residence of the harbourmaster. Today it is two private homes.

Northern Djurgården, too, was part of the royal hunting park where Charles XI had hunted in the 17th century. The photo shows a meadow near Stora Skuggan, a summer house. The cottage is known as Charles XI's fishing hut (17th c.).

The Environs

What a visitor might regard as the city's surroundings are today either part of the city itself, or else form separate municipalities.

Greater Stockholm is in fact made up of twenty such »communes», of which some have grown together with the city and some even form part of its central areas.

These photos are taken either in the western or southern outskirts, or in the neighbouring municipalities. Waldemarsudde, on the shore of Djurgården, must stand for the whole Archipelago, that vast holiday paradise, with its thousands of islands and wonderful sailing waters.

Haga and Hagalund both form part of the town of Solna. Lidingö and Huddinge are both independent communes, as is Ekerö in the Mälaren region, which also comprises Drottningholm. Vällingby, Farsta and Skärholmen are all part of Stockholm City.

Prince Eugen's Waldemarsudde was built 1903-04, to plans by architect Ferdinand Boberg. Its picture gallery was added in 1913 and extended in 1945. Here the prince, brother of Gustav V, had his own studio. The entrance to Stockholm harbour, with the archipelago steamers coming and going, was one of his favourite motifs.

In the 1780's Gustaf III (1772-92) erected pavilions and pleasure palaces in Haga Park. It was then the Haga pavilion and the so-called Copper Tents (photo) were built, from designs by the French architect L.J. Desprez. Haga Palace (photo; 1802-1804, architect C.C. Gjörwell) was originally called the Queen's Pavilion. Today it is a residence for visiting statesmen. Gustaf III never realised his plans for a large palace at Haga. All that remains of the works, begun in 1786, is a few ruins.

Drottningholm Palace, designed by Nicodemus Tessin snr., built 1662-1699. Its wings were added in the mid-18th century. The gardens were designed by the younger Tessin. Drottningholm is also famous for its unique – and still functioning – Court Theatre (1764-1766), and for the »China» Pavilion, a birthday present to Queen Lovisa Ulrika, sister of Frederick the Great, in 1753.

Djursholm is still a well-to-do suburb. When its villas began to be built in the 1890's it lay far outside the city boundaries. This villa in Tulevägen is typical.

In 1906 the sculptor Carl Milles purchased a rather inaccessible cliff on the island of Lidingö. Two years later he built himself a house and a studio. Gradually Millesgården grew into a large outdoor museum, where virtually the whole of Milles' oeuvre can be seen – either originals or in replica. Also his personal collection of works of art from various periods.

Hagalund was another late 19th-century Stockholm suburb. Villas in the then so popular »Swiss» style were built on land parcelled out from a manor. This pale blue house, once the home of the painter Olle Olsson-Hagalund (virtually all that is left of the quaint idyll of former days) was built by the painter's grandfather, a carpenter, in the 1890's.

Eight identical 14-storey apartment blocks have swept away old Hagalund — the locals call them »Blåkulla», the witches mountain. But the painter could paint no more.

After World War II Stockholm began to expand swiftly far beyond its traditional limits. Whole new suburbs began to spring up where there had always been only fields and forest. Vällingby, developed in the 1950's, is a satellite town, with its own traffic-free shopping centre.

To the south of the capital lie two more satellite towns: Farsta Centrum, (early 1960's) and Skärholmen, with its vast underground car park (late 1960's).

The suburban idyll is everywhere being transformed; e.g., by the huge Huddinge Hospital, built in the 1970's and by new housing blocks nearby, at Västra Flemingsberg (photo).